Happy Birthday, Dear Jesus!

ST. LOUIS DE MONTFORT
11441 HAGUE ROAD
FISHERS, IN 46038

by Greg Holder and Diane Stortz
illustrated by Terri Steiger

STANDARD
PUBLISHING
Cincinnati, Ohio

© 1995, The Standard Publishing Company, Cincinnati, Ohio
A division of Standex International Corporation. Printed in U.S.A. All rights reserved.
Library of Congress CIP data available. Designed by Coleen Davis. ISBN 0-7847-0354-X

Christmas is coming,
and we're planning
a party —
a birthday party!

You can help us get
ready.
There's lots to do!

This party is special,
because it's for the
most important
birthday of all —

Jesus'
birthday!

First, we put up decorations . . .

all over the house!

Then we decorate the tree,
with tiny twinkling lights, bright paper chains . . .

shiny silver bells, and a glowing golden star.
We think our trees are *beautiful!*

Christmas cards
are fun to sign
and send to all
our friends.

"It's Jesus' birthday!"
is what the cards say.

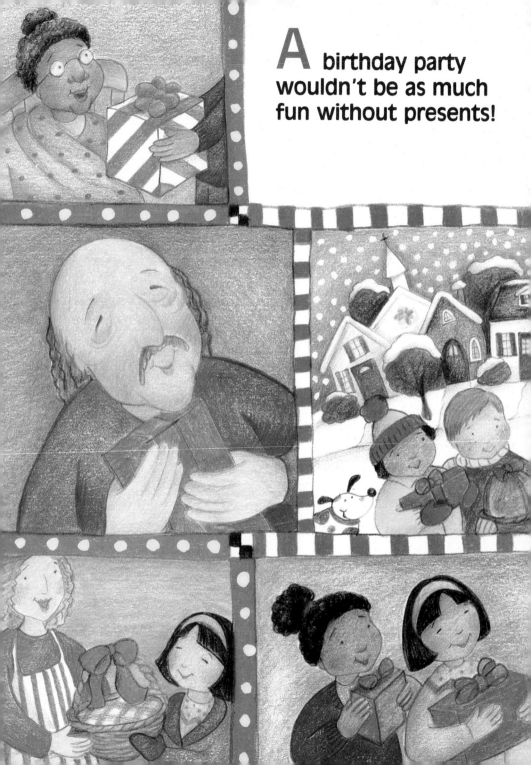

A birthday party wouldn't be as much fun without presents!

Our birthday gifts
for Jesus
are the things
we do for others.

We give gifts
to each other, too!

We wrap them and
tie them and stack them
under the tree.

Come into the kitchen now.
It's time to make Jesus' birthday cake!

CRACK! PLOP! WHIRR-R-R-R!
We stir and stir.

After the cake bakes in the oven, we let it cool.

Then we
swirl sweet,
fluffy frosting
up, down,
and all around,
and we write
"Happy Birthday, Jesus"
on the top.

But we can't eat yet!
There's one more thing to do,
one more very important thing . . .

We open the Bible and read about Jesus – God's Son – lying in a manger, and angels praising God, and shepherds hurrying to Bethlehem to visit the special baby.

Welcome, carolers! Please come in

e're having a party
r the most important
thday of all —

Jesus'
birthday!
And we have one more
song to sing . . .